Philosophy in the Classroom

T

Ever had difficul   inspiring your children to consider and discuss philosophical concepts

Philosophy in t   assroom helps teachers tap in to children's natural wonder
and curiosity.   practical lesson plans, built around Aesop's fables,
encourage childr   formulate and express their own points of view, enabl-
ing you to lead r   d rewarding philosophical discussions in the primary
classroom.

This highly pr   d engaging classroom companion:

- Prompts stu   nsider serious moral issues in an imaginative and
  stimulating
- Uses Aesop's   as a springboard to pose challenging questions about
  the issues rai
- Provides 15   themes including happiness, wisdom, self-reliance
  and judging   s as the basis for classroom discussion.
- Uses power   d creative drawings to illustrate activities and
  photocopiab   urces.

Philosophy   th   om is an invaluable resource for any primary school
teacher wa   g to engage their students in meaningful philosophical
reflection and discussion.

Ron Shaw has many years of classroom experience and is the author of more
than 40 books helping primary and secondary school students to improve
their thinking skills.

Philosophy in the Classroom

Improving your pupils' thinking skills and motivating them to learn

Ron Shaw

Routledge
Taylor & Francis Group

LONDON AND NEW YORK

First published 2003
by Curriculum Corporation, Australia
reprinted in 2003
This edition published 2008
by Routledge
2 Park Square, Milton Park, Abingdon, Oxon OX14 4RN

Simultaneously published in the USA and Canada
by Routledge
270 Madison Ave, New York, NY 10016

Routledge is an imprint of the Taylor & Francis Group, an informa business

© 2008 Ron Shaw

Typeset in Garamond and Helvetica by
RefineCatch Limited, Bungay, Suffolk
Printed and bound in Great Britain by
TJ International Ltd, Padstow, Cornwall

British Library Cataloguing in Publication Data
A catalogue record for this book is available from the British Library

Library of Congress Cataloging in Publication Data
Shaw, Ron.
   Philosophy in the classroom: improving your pupils' thinking
skills and motivating them to learn / Ron Shaw.
        p. cm.
   1. Critical thinking in children – Study and teaching (Primary) 2.
Creative thinking in children – Study and teaching (Primary) 3.
Motivation in education. I. Title.
   LB1590.3.S43 2008
   370.15'2 – dc22
   2007020500

Artwork by Mark Fox

ISBN10: 0–415–44710–0 (pbk)
ISBN10: 0–203–93574–8 (ebk)

ISBN13: 978–0–415–44710–2 (pbk)
ISBN13: 978–0–203–93574–3 (ebk)

Contents

Introduction

Welcome to *Philosophy in the Classroom*.

The book was conceived with a view to improving students' thinking skills by encouraging them to take part in interesting discussions.

Thinking can be 'skills' oriented, as in teaching the difference between fact and opinion, or how to make a valid generalisation. Alternatively, it can be 'organic' and holistic – mental stimulation generated naturally in grappling with a real-life problem or everyday issue. This course in thinking fits into the latter approach. It offers students a 'thinking problem' in the most palatable form: a story exploring a key issue. The story is short (one of Aesop's traditional fables) and the issue is obvious. All the work (and benefit) is in exploring the key issue. Questions are provided to guide discussion, and a set of 'provocative' proverbs is added, as an additional stimulus to thought.

It is up to the teacher to manage the classroom use of their material as he/she thinks fit. Some of these talks and conversations will work best in small group settings, while others lend themselves more to the involvement of every student in the class at once.

Many of the quotes in this book use masculine words: 'He who . . .'; 'Happy is the man who . . .'. For simplicity it has been decided to leave these as they are, rather than to alter them to gender-neutral.

I trust that you and your pupils will enjoy the stories and discussion topics that follow.

The involvement of all children in the discussions can lead to only one outcome – enhanced thinking skills in the classroom.

The benefits to all other subject areas are self-evident.

Ron Shaw

Teachers' Notes

Background to teaching philosophy to children

Philosophers in Greece were known as 'friends of wisdom', or as those who cultivated excellence in thinking. The word 'philosophy' comes from the Greek words *philo* (cover) and *sophos* (wisdom). Philosophy is quite simply the study of knowledge (or truth).

But for 2500 years philosophy was thought to be too difficult a subject for children to study. It was therefore restricted to courses in the colleges and universities.

Socrates was a Greek philosopher who used many forms of oral questioning in teaching his pupils. Socrates believed that questions were the source of knowledge. **Socratic dialogue** is a dialogue consisting of a series of oral questions posed by the instructor to promote the cognitive process in students. The process of Socratic dialogue assists students to organise their thoughts and sequence their learning. It guides learning by emphasising what is important and relevant.

The teacher asks a series of questions that leads the students to examine the validity of an opinion or belief. This is a powerful teaching method because it actively engages the learner and forces critical thinking, which is just what is needed in examining ethics, values and other social or humane issues. The method is also dramatic and entertaining, and it triggers lively classroom discussion.

Mathew Lipman, the American pioneer (and 'guru') of Philosophy for Children was inspired by the philosopher and educationist John Dewey, who envisaged a classroom community of students engaging co-operatively in learning, motivated by their own curiosity and sense of wonder. Dewey and Lipman believed that such classrooms educated children to be responsible and active participants in society.

The distinctive approach of Philosophy for Children lies in its assumption that reasoning skills are best developed when young people are involved in open-ended, peer group discussions of ideas in which they themselves are interested.

Why teach philosophy to children?

Philosophy is a marvellous source of motivation. We need to make use of it. Children are curious and exhibit great wonder about the world. We count on that natural curiosity to create questions and develop an enquiry. We seek to tap children's wonder to help them formulate and express their own points of view. It is the singularity of each child's experience that makes philosophical discussions so rich. Philosophy for Children presupposes great trust in children. We trust that they have natural capacities to wonder and think and imagine. These are the capacities necessary for genuine learning.

Philosophy in the Classroom aims to improve reasoning abilities of students, improve the quality of student thinking about important matters and examine ethical issues.

While some teachers find 'values classification' a problematic area, few would dispute the goal of having children become more thoughtful, responsible and with a sound understanding of behaviours society considers worthwhile, as opposed to those behaviours considered undesirable. These are goals, too, of Philosophy for Children.

Advantages of teaching philosophy to children

- Philosophy for Children sharpens children's linguistic, logical and cognitive competence. The classroom dialogue is something students find irresistible: they can't help joining in, contributing their own reflections to the discussion. In this way, cognitive skilfulness is acquired in context, rather than in isolated drills. Extensive testing, particularly at the year 5–8 level, has repeatedly demonstrated participation in a philosophy programme to have significant impact on **improving basic skills**, performance in other subject areas and **readiness for learning** generally.
- Philosophy provides students with **skills of enquiry**, to help them **understand the world** and their experience of it, both in and out of school, so that they might become more **thoughtful, articulate and reasonable human beings**.
- It is in discussions that children develop the habits of alertness and **skilful, considerate thinking**. And just as language is learned more readily in play, Philosophy for Children helps students to learn to reason well in discussions where they are free from having to come up with predetermined results. Open-ended discussion allows them to follow up and explore their own ideas in relation to those of others. The students deliberate among themselves, and this process of deliberation is then internalised by the individual students: they become more reflective and begin to think for themselves. These classroom deliberations evoke thinking that is skilful and deliberate, thinking that employs relevant criteria, is self-correcting, and is sensitive to context. It is not just any kind of thinking, it is critical thinking.
- Philosophy is valuable socially. The programme does not attempt to

inculcate any particular philosophical theory or viewpoint – only good reasoning. Rather than impede, participants' differences enrich the inquiry. Through thinking, talking, listening and questioning together, and respecting other ideas, children develop **mutual co-operation, trust, care, respect** ... and much more. Because the Socratic method triggers fruitful group discussions, children get to see how their peers are thinking and feeling about important issues. Very often, they are relieved to learn that others are having the same thoughts and feelings as they are.

- Philosophy taps into children's natural curiosity and wonder, and is **relevant across the curriculum.** Many of the principles discussed (e.g. co-operation, respect for the truth) are of universal application. It engages students in the search for meaning as well as strengthening their thinking and reasoning skills and enriching their understanding. An important focus is on fostering young people's confidence and self-esteem.

- Philosophy is good **preparation for life.** By discussing real-life dilemmas now, we are preparing students to make better choices in the future. The Socratic method has been shown to be a highly effective approach for helping children become ethical, respectful, responsible people who think critically, solve problems non-violently and make choices based on what's right instead of what they can get away with.

- Philosophy involves **personal growth.** Children often see the problem with 'fresh eyes' and soon learn that modifying their previously held views can be a sign of newly-acquired wisdom.

Teaching hints

1. Discussions can take place with students seated at their classroom desks. However, a better arrangement is for everyone to be <u>sitting in a circle</u>. A retreat setting removed from competing interests and using smaller groups of students is ideal.

2. Be comfortable with the fact that **the teacher does not know** at the beginning of the session **where the discussion will lead the group,** and is not in control of where the class ends up at the conclusion of the session. The **teacher** is a **facilitator** or **co-inquirer** who is responsible for the form of the discussion, rather than the content.

3. Make the students take a position, by asking open-ended questions. You might start with:

   'What would you do if . . .?'

   Complicate the situation by throwing in a question such as:

   'What if this happened, what would you do then?'

   At each step, raise the ante:

   'Now what would you do?'
   'Would that be the **right** thing to do?'

   A consensus will probably develop. The children will usually know what's right when pressed. If you ask children what they would do in a certain situation, their responses will range from noble and altruistic to selfish and calculating. But if you then ask them what's the right thing to do, a consensus develops.

Kids usually know what's right, they just need the confidence and the encouragement to act on it.

4. **Give something** of yourself – share something **personal**. Don't just take. Let the students know you don't have all the answers, that you, too, have fears and insecurities. Be honest with the students.

5. Take a **non-judgemental attitude**. It is important to appear non-judgemental, so that your students feel safe in expressing their ideas. Without their *true* thoughts and feelings on the table, the dialogue is pointless. However, you should not give the impression that anything they may conclude is okay, or that all conclusions are equally valid.

6. Listen. Take the students seriously and **show respect** for their thoughts and opinions. When necessary, disagree respectfully.

7. **Keep the discussion focused**. Don't allow it to drift off into 'free association' storytelling.

8. **Keep the discussion intellectually responsible**. If someone makes what is clearly a prejudicial or factually incorrect assertation, gently remind the class that 'That is a myth' or 'There is no proof for that, so we shouldn't believe it to be true'.

9. Periodically **summarise** what has and what has not been dealt with and/or resolved.

10. **Draw as many students** as possible into the discussion. Guard against particular individuals dominating. Protect anyone whose opinion might be seen as marginalised, or worse, degraded.

11. Encourage students to provide an **example** or two where appropriate.

12. Don't accept, 'I don't agree' by itself – reasons must be given. This encourages the idea of intellectual rigour.

13. Encourage **idea generation** and problem solving. Explore many possible solutions to a problem.

14. Encourage flexibility and no blame, no guilt modification of existing attitudes. It is understood that changing one's mind about one's views is often part of the process of philosophical thinking.

15. **Assessment** is by participation, thoughtfulness and quality of responses. Assessment should not be based on 'having the right opinion', but on how fully a student has participated and how much mental energy has gone into the discussion. There should be no winners or losers in philosophy – only wiser people.

16. While the exercises in this book are predominantly discussion-based, teachers may choose to elicit **written responses** in certain cases. Some exercises may even be given as home assignments.

HAPPINESS

The Father and His Two Daughters

A man had two daughters. One was married to a gardener, and the other to a tile maker. After a time the man went to the daughter who had married the gardener, and inquired how she was and how all things went with her. She said, 'All things are prospering with me. I have only one wish, that there may be a heavy fall of rain, in order that the plants may be well watered.' Not long after, he went to the daughter who had married the tile maker, and likewise inquired of her how she fared. She replied, 'I want for nothing, and have only one wish, that the dry weather may continue, and the sun shine hot and bright, so that the bricks might be dried.' He said to her, 'If your sister wishes for rain, and you for dry weather, with which of the two am I to join my wishes?'

Moral of the story:
You can't please everybody.

Thinking, Reasoning and Discussing

Question 1. Can you think of anything which would have brought happiness to both daughters in the story?

....

....

Question 2. Can you think of any people in society whose jobs require them to make decisions that are sure to please only some people, while displeasing others?

....

....

Question 3. Have you ever found yourself in a situation where *you* could not please everyone?

....

....

Question 4. If you have to make a decision where you know not everyone will be pleased, what could you do to make the situation better?

....

....

Question 5. Should you *always* try to please as many people as you can?

....

....

Question 6. What's worse – telling a lie and pleasing everyone, or telling the truth and pleasing no one?

....

....

....

Question 7. Suppose two of your friends, whom you like equally, both invite you to their house for a sleepover on the same night. These friends of yours happen to be not so friendly with each other. Say what you would do, and mention the factors that would influence your decision.

....

....

....

Philosophy in the Classroom © Ron Shaw, Routledge 2008

In 'The Father and His Two Daughters', the father was not able to bring **happiness** to both of his daughters.

Here are some more questions about happiness to consider:

- What is happiness?

- Do happy parents have happy children?

- Is it possible to be totally happy all of the time?

- What brings happiness?

- What takes away happiness?

- Is it true that we would rather be surrounded by happy people than by sad people? Explain your answer.

- Is it possible to be happy even when you're surrounded by unhappy people?

- Is it possible to be unhappy even when you're surrounded by happy people?

- Are some people born happier than others? If so, why?

- Is it possible to have few possessions and no money and still be happy?

- Can someone be happy while feeling ill?

- Who is more likely to be happy – a person who knows little, or a person who knows a lot?

- One person has many talents but is poor. Another person has no talents but is wealthy. Who do you think would be happier?

- Is happiness more or less important than health?

Provocative Proverbs: Happiness

Make happy those who are near, and those who are far will come.
CHINESE PROVERB

Why do the Chinese think that 'those who are far will come' if we make happy those who are near?

Happiness you pay for is to be found everywhere.
GYPSY PROVERB

What could the gypsies have meant by this?

True happiness lies in giving it to others.
INDIAN PROVERB

Do you agree with this proverb?

Can you think of anything, apart from happiness, that you gain by giving to others?

There is no winter without snow, no spring without sunshine, and no happiness without companions.
KOREAN PROVERB

This proverb seems to say that in order to have happiness we need companions. Do you agree?

A happy man does not hear the clock strike.
GERMAN PROVERB

What might the Germans mean by this proverb?

Happiness is a horse. You have to harness it.
RUSSIAN PROVERB

What is meant by this proverb? Why must happiness be harnessed?

Debate Topic
It's better to be happy than wise.

KINDNESS

The Hares and the Frogs

The Hares, concerned by their own exceeding timidity and weary of the perpetual alarm to which they were exposed, determined to put an end to themselves and their troubles by jumping from a lofty cliff into a deep lake below. As they scampered off in large numbers to carry out their plan, the Frogs lying on the banks of the lake heard the noise of their feet and rushed helter-skelter to the deep water for safety. On seeing the rapid disappearance of the Frogs, one of the Hares cried out to his companions: 'Stay, my friends. Do not do as you intended. For you now see that there are creatures who are still more timid than ourselves.'

Moral of the story:
There is always someone worse off than yourself.

Thinking, Reasoning and Discussing

Question 1. The hare changed his mind about jumping from the cliff when he saw someone more timid than himself. Why do you think this made him change his mind?

....

Question 2. Can being timid *ever* be to a person's advantage?

....

Question 3. Does it help to know there is someone worse off than yourself? Why/Why not?

....

Question 4. When you come across someone who is worse off than you are, do you feel like helping them? If yes, why?

....

Question 5. Do you think you need to suffer a misfortune to really understand the suffering of someone with that same misfortune?

....

Question 6. Are we more likely to want to help those whose sufferings we can easily identify with?

....

Question 7. If things are not going well for us, we may feel sorry for ourselves. Do we just as easily feel that we are lucky when things go our way? Which is the stronger feeling?

....

....

Question 8. Can you think of a time when you felt sorry for yourself, but then realised there was someone worse off than you? Did it have any effect on the way you felt?

....

....

Question 9. Suppose you told your friend that your bike had been stolen. Your friend then says that their house was burgled and that everyone lost precious possessions. How would you feel? How would you react? What would you say?

....

....

Philosophy in the Classroom © Ron Shaw, Routledge 2008

In 'The Hares and the Frogs', one of the Hares showed **kindness** and compassion by not wanting to frighten the Frogs.

Here are some more questions about kindness to consider:

- What is meant by kindness?

- Is it ever *wrong* to be kind?

- Are animals capable of acts of kindness towards other animals?

- Are animals capable of acts of kindness towards humans?

- Does being kind require effort?

- Can kindness have any disadvantages?

- Who benefits more from an act of kindness, the giver or the receiver?

- Is it possible for a person to be both kind *and* selfish?

- Is it possible for a person who has little wealth and few material possessions to be as kind as a person who has much wealth and many material possessions?

- Does kindness always involve helping someone?

- Does kindness always involve thinking of others?

- Which is better – being kind to others, or being kind to animals?

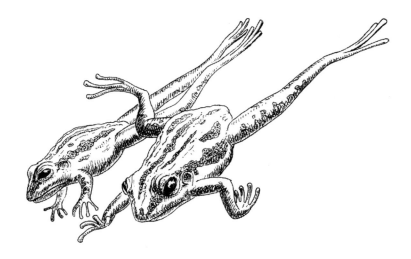

Provocative Proverbs: Kindness

Do not forget little kindnesses and do not remember small faults.
CHINESE PROVERB

Change the places of the words 'kindnesses' and 'faults' in this proverb. Do you think there are people who follow the 'new' proverb? Could anyone be happy in a world where everyone did this?

Write injuries in sand, kindnesses in marble.
FRENCH PROVERB

Explain why the words 'sand' and 'marble' are used in this proverb. Is this proverb a useful one?

One can pay back the loan of gold, but one lies forever in debt to those who are kind.
MALAYSIAN PROVERB

The Malays say it is easier to repay a large loan of money than an act of kindness. Do you agree?

With a sweet tongue of kindness, you can drag an elephant by a hair.
PERSIAN PROVERB

What might the Persians have meant by this proverb?

Kindness begets kindness.
GREEK PROVERB

Can you explain this proverb?

The greatest wisdom of all is kindness.
HEBREW PROVERB

Why might the Hebrews say that being kind shows great wisdom?

Sometimes you must be cruel to be kind.
ENGLISH PROVERB

Can you think of a situation when this proverb might apply?

One joy scatters a hundred griefs.
CHINESE PROVERB

Say how this proverb applies to kindness.

> **Debate Topic**
> **It's always better to think of others before ourselves.**

JUDGEMENT

The Ant and the Chrysalis

An Ant nimbly running about in the sunshine in search of food came across a Chrysalis that was very near its time of change. The Chrysalis moved its tail, and thus attracted the attention of the Ant, who saw for the first time that it was alive. 'Poor, pitiable animal!' cried the Ant disdainfully. 'What a sad fate is yours! While I can run hither and thither, at my pleasure, and, if I wish, climb the tallest tree, you lie imprisoned here in your shell, with power only to move a joint or two of your scaly tail.' The Chrysalis heard all this, but did not try to make any reply. A few days later, when the Ant passed that way again, nothing but the shell remained. Wondering what had become of its contents, he felt himself suddenly shaded and fanned by the gorgeous wings of a beautiful Butterfly. 'Behold in me,' said the Butterfly, 'your much-pitied friend! Boast now of your powers to run and climb as long as you can get me to listen.' So saying, the Butterfly rose in the air, and, borne along and aloft on the summer breeze, was soon lost to the sight of the Ant forever.

Moral of the story:
Appearances are deceptive.

Thinking, Reasoning and Discussing

Question 1. What attitude did the Ant have, and how does the fable imply it should be judged?

....

Question 2. Unlike the Chrysalis the Ant was able to move about freely. Was the Ant able to move about as freely as the Butterfly?

....

Question 3. Can you think of other living things (animal, bird, insect, plant) about which it could be said 'appearances are deceptive'?

....

Question 4. Do you know anyone about whom it could be said 'appearances are deceptive'?

....

Question 5. Are appearances *always* deceptive?

....

Question 6. What can we do to ensure that we are not deceived by appearances?

....

Question 7. Can you think of a time when you or someone else was fooled by someone's or something's appearance?

....

Question 8. If something looks good, is it more likely to be judged favourably?

....

Question 9. If someone looks good, are they more likely to be respected and trusted?

....

Question 10. Some say the great white shark, despite its ominous appearance, is a magnificent creature, yet it has also been described as a ruthless killing machine. Can it be *both* these things?

....

Question 11. Is a well-dressed, well-groomed person more or less likely to be kind and generous than a person of shabby appearance?

....

Question 12. Is appearance important and/or overrated?

....

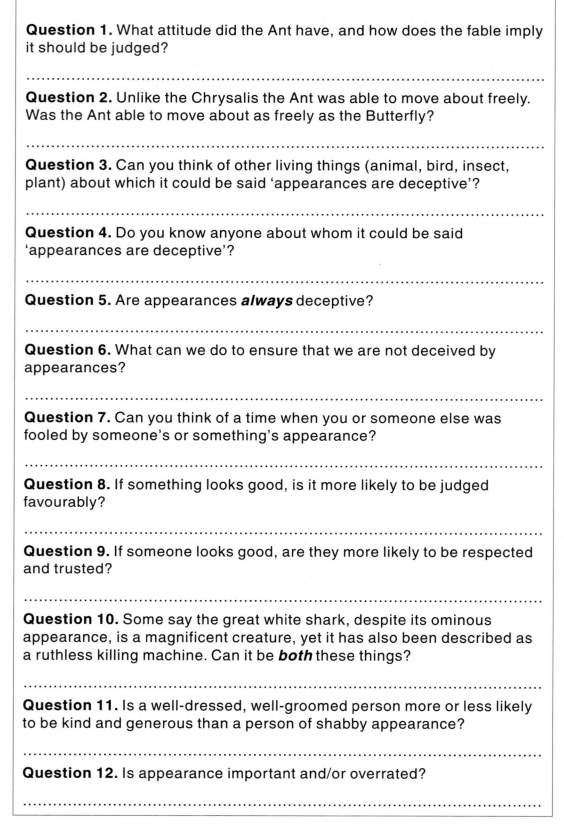

Philosophy in the Classroom © Ron Shaw, Routledge 2008

In 'The Ant and the Chrysalis', the Ant made a false **judgement** about the Chrysalis.

Here are some more questions about judgement to consider:

- What is judgement?

- Does judgement always involve making decisions?

- Are judgements always *either* right *or* wrong?

- What is needed to make a good judgement?

- Can two people make a different judgement of the same thing and *both* be right?

- What makes one judgement better than another?

- Is it easier to make judgements about ourselves or others?

- Do animals make judgements?

- Why might we make different judgements about the *same* thing at different times?

- If two judgements are different, is one better than the other?

- Can we make a judgement without using any of our senses?

- Do we make judgements every day?

- How are judgements different from opinions?

Provocative Proverbs: Judgement

You can't see the whole sky through a bamboo tube.
JAPANESE PROVERB

How does this proverb apply to making judgements?

The cobra will bite you, whether you call it cobra or Mr Cobra.
INDIAN PROVERB

What were the Indians thinking when they created this proverb?

Words have no wings but they can fly many thousands of miles.
SOUTH KOREAN PROVERB

What can this teach us about what we tell others?

Who lies with dogs shall rise up with fleas.
LATIN PROVERB

Does this proverb caution us about friendships? What is it saying?

What you cannot avoid, welcome.
CHINESE PROVERB

Why should we choose to welcome what we cannot avoid?

Debate Topic
Making judgements of people based on their appearance is unwise.

POWER

The North Wind and the Sun

The North Wind and the Sun argued as to which was the most powerful, and agreed that he should be declared the victor who could first strip a wayfaring man of his clothes. The North Wind first tried his power and blew with all his might, but the keener his blasts, the closer the Traveller wrapped his cloak around him, until at last, giving up all hope of victory, the Wind called upon the Sun to see what he could do. The Sun suddenly shone out with all his warmth. The Traveller no sooner felt his genial rays than he took off one garment after another, and at last, fairly overcome with heat, undressed and bathed in a stream that lay in his path.

Moral of the story:
Persuasion is better than force.

Thinking, Reasoning and Discussing

Question 1. Explain in simple language why this fable has its moral.

....

....

Question 2. When people try to force us to do something, do we usually resist?

....

Question 3. Is persuasion always better than force?

....

....

Question 4. Which has the most chance of succeeding – force that has failed, followed by persuasion; or persuasion that has failed, followed by force?

....

....

Question 5. Can you think of a time when failed persuasion had to be followed by force? If not, try to think of a situation where this could occur.

....

....

Question 6. Can you think of a time when failed force had to be followed by persuasion? If not, try to think of a situation where this could occur.

....

....

Question 7. Are there some people with whom force works better than persuasion?

....

Question 8. Which two of the following words **do not** go with persuasion: reward, threat, promise, incentive, harm, coax?

....

Question 9. Do you think anyone should ever be forced to do anything?

....

Question 10. Which is the more powerful – force or persuasion?

....

Philosophy in the Classroom © Ron Shaw, Routledge 2008

In 'The North Wind and the Sun', the North Wind thought it had more **power** than the Sun.

Here are some more questions about power to consider:

- What is power?

- What kinds of power are there?

- Is it good to have power?

- Does *everyone* enjoy having power?

- Is power the same as strength?

- Can a poor person have as much power as a rich person?

- What makes a person powerful?

- Can people give power to others?

- What is the opposite of power?

- Are there disadvantages to being a person who has power?

- Is it better to have total power, some power or no power?

- Can small people have as much power as bigger people?

- What kinds of power can animals have?

- A nation may be described as powerful. What does this mean?

- Who or what else, apart from the things mentioned above, can have power?

- How is power gained?

- How is power lost?

Provocative Proverbs: Power

The wolf loses his teeth, but not his inclinations.

SPANISH PROVERB

Can the wolf still be menacing after it loses its teeth?

A little axe can cut down a big tree.

JAMAICAN PROVERB

A little fire burns up a great deal of corn.

HEBREW PROVERB

These two proverbs are saying the same thing. What is it?

If there were no elephant in the jungle, the buffalo would be a great animal.

GHANAIAN PROVERB

What are the Ghanaians saying here?

The pen is mightier than the sword.

GREEK PROVERB

How can this be?

A friend in power is a friend lost.

SCOTTISH PROVERB

Is this a proverb about power, friendship or both? What is it saying?

Hares play freely near the body of a dead lion.

GREEK PROVERB

What does this proverb have to do with power?

> **Debate Topic**
> **A powerful group will always defeat a powerful individual.**

CO-OPERATION

The Bundle of Sticks

An old man on the point of death summoned his sons around him to give them some parting advice. He ordered his servants to bring in a bundle of sticks, and said to his eldest son, 'Break it.' The son strained and strained, but for all his efforts was unable to break the bundle. The other sons also tried, but neither of them was successful. 'Untie the bundle,' said the father, 'and each of you take a stick.' When they had done so, he called out to them, 'Now, break.' And each stick was easily broken. 'You see my meaning,' said their father.

Moral of the story:
Union gives strength.

Thinking, Reasoning and Discussing

Question 1. Two morals can be taken from this fable. One has been given. What is the other (opposite) moral?

....

Question 2. How could the word 'union' be applied to this story?

....

Question 3. How does the moral of the bundle of sticks apply to all of the sons?

....

Question 4. Can you think of times when two or more people acting together achieved more than one person acting alone?

....

....

Question 5. Can you think of any circumstances where the union of two or more persons could result in *less* strength than when one of those people works alone?

....

....

Question 6. Which is stronger – one person acting alone, or a union of persons (one of whom is weak) acting together?

....

Question 7. Do you think 'union gives strength' is true only in the case of people? Can you think of cases, not involving people, where 'union gives strength' is true?

....

....

Question 8. Try to recall a circumstance in your life where 'union gives strength' held true.

....

Question 9. See if you can think of a circumstance in nature where 'union gives strength' applies.

....

Question 10. Can you can think of anything in the non-living world where 'union gives strength' applies?

....

In 'The Bundle of Sticks', the father relied on the **co-operation** of his sons.

Here are some more questions about co-operation to consider:

- What is meant by co-operation?

- When is co-operation important/needed?

- Do animals ever co-operate with each other?

- Is someone who doesn't co-operate a bad person?

- Is it *always* good to co-operate?

- Is it ever wrong to co-operate?

- Is 'co-operation' the same thing as 'joining in'?

- Can co-operation ever be a sign of weakness?

- Is it ever okay to *force* someone to co-operate?

- How is 'co-operation' different from 'conformity'?

- Does co-operation ever get in the way of individuality?

- Would a sporting team of highly talented individuals who don't co-operate well with one another during the match defeat a team of less talented players who co-operate well with one another?

- What is the difference in meaning between 'co-operate' and 'help'?

Provocative Proverbs: Co-operation

If all pulled in one direction, the world would keel over.
HEBREW PROVERB

When people co-operate with one another, much energy and power can be generated. Is this energy and power always positive though? Give examples.

One rotten apple spoils the barrel.
IRISH PROVERB

How does this proverb apply to co-operation?

A chain is only as strong as its weakest link.
SCOTTISH PROVERB

Can you explain this proverb and suggest how it has relevance to co-operation?

Divide the fire and you will soon put it out.
GREEK PROVERB

Give an example from real life to say how an unco-operative individual can 'put the fire out'.

Many hands make light work.
ENGLISH PROVERB

This proverb is about sharing the load. Is co-operation always about sharing the load? If not, what else is it about?

When spider webs unite, they can tie up a lion.
ETHIOPIAN PROVERB

Can you see what this has to do with co-operation? Can you think of an example which proves the wisdom of this proverb?

Debate Topic
No one should ever be forced to co-operate.

VANITY

The Fir Tree and the Bramble

A Fir Tree said boastingly to the Bramble, 'You are useful for nothing at all, while I am used everywhere for roofs and houses.' The Bramble answered: 'You poor creature, if you would only call to mind the axes and saws which are about to hew you down, you would have reason to wish that you had grown up a Bramble, not a Fir Tree.'

Moral of the story:
Better poverty without care than riches with.

Thinking, Reasoning and Discussing

Question 1. If you were the Fir Tree, what might you have said next?

....

Question 2. Who might have the better life, the Fir Tree or the Bramble?

....

Question 3. The Fir Tree boasts about its uses and seems to consider itself superior to the Bramble. Would you say the Fir Tree is conceited, proud or both?

....

Question 4. Is it better to be conceited or modest?

....

Question 5. Would you say that this story shows that it is not always a good thing to be in demand? Give other examples you know of.

....

....

Question 6. The Fir Tree has more beauty and more uses than the Bramble but who would you say possesses the most wisdom? Discuss.

....

....

Question 7. Can you think of anyone you have known who boasted about things they own or things they were good at? Why do you think they did this?

....

....

Question 8. When someone boasts, what effects can it have on those who hear it?

....

Question 9. Is beauty or wisdom more important?

....

Question 10. Are you better off being rich and having no cares, or being poor with no cares?

....

....

Philosophy in the Classroom © Ron Shaw, Routledge 2008

In 'The Fir Tree and the Bramble', the Fir Tree showed its **vanity** by boasting about its uses.

Here are some more questions about vanity to consider:

- What is vanity?
- Is it normal *sometimes* to be vain?
- If someone doesn't boast does that mean they're not vain?
- Can vanity *ever* be good?
- Is it possible to be vain and have respect for others?
- Is it possible to be vain and have no self-confidence?
- Do vain people think highly of themselves in everything or only in some things?
- Are people born vain or do they become vain?
- What causes vanity?
- Can a vain person lose their vanity? If so, say how.
- With which kind of people do vain people form friendships?
- Does vanity have any advantages?
- Does vanity have any disadvantages?
- Could a person be vain if they never saw any other people?
- Is vanity the same as self-love?
- Is it possible to be vain and wish you weren't?

Provocative Proverbs: Vanity

Boasting begins where wisdom stops.
JAPANESE PROVERB

What do the Japanese mean here?

Do not mend your neighbour's fence before seeing to your own.
TANZANIAN PROVERB

Do you think that vanity is sometimes accompanied by finding fault with others?

What could a vain person learn from this proverb?

If a word be worth one shekel, silence is worth two.
HEBREW PROVERB

Speech is silver; silence is golden.
SWISS PROVERB

These proverbs are both about silence.

Why should people who are vain take heed of these words?

The tallest blade of grass is the first to be cut by the scythe.
RUSSIAN PROVERB

Say how the Russians may have been thinking about vanity when they made up this proverb.

The trees with most leaves will not necessarily produce juicy fruit.
BRAZILIAN PROVERB

Say how this proverb relates to vanity.

Debate Topic
A vain person can never be a nice person.

PLEASURE AND PAIN

The Boys and the Frogs

Some Boys, playing near a pond, saw a number of Frogs in the water and began to pelt them with stones. They killed several of them. Then one of the Frogs, lifting his head out of the water, cried out, 'Pray stop, my boys. What is sport to you, is death to us.'

Moral of the story:
One man's pleasure may be another's pain.

Thinking, Reasoning and Discussing

Question 1. Would you say that the Boys thought about the pain they inflicted on the Frogs?

....

Question 2. If frogs could really talk do you think the Boys would have thrown rocks at them? If you think 'no', why wouldn't they?

....

Question 3. What is it about killing frogs with rocks that could give pleasure to someone?

....

Question 4. Are people more likely to harm non-human creatures than their fellow humans?

....

Question 5. Are people more likely to harm frogs than dogs? Give reasons for your answer.

....

....

Question 6. Can you think of an example of 'one man's pleasure is another man's pain' that does not involve physical or emotional abuse'?

....

Question 7. Can you think of anything that can give pleasure to some but has the opposite effect on others? ***Examples:*** *a school subject; a food type; a particular movie.*

....

Question 8. Sky diving and bungy jumping give pleasure to some. Name some other pursuits that bring pleasure to thrill-seekers, yet cause others to experience anxiety.

....

....

Question 9. Can you think of something you really enjoyed that had a negative effect on someone else?

....

Question 10. Can you think of something that had a negative effect on you that someone else found pleasurable?

....

In 'The Boys and the Frogs', the Boys' **pleasure** was obtained by causing **pain** to the Frogs.

Here are some more questions about pleasure and pain to consider:

- What is pleasure?

- What are some things that bring pleasure to people?

- If something that you experience today brings you pleasure, will that same thing bring you pleasure if experienced in the future?

- Can pleasure be physical, or is it only to do with thoughts and feelings?

- Are 'pleasure' and 'happiness' the same thing?

- When/how/why does a feeling of pleasure stop?

- If something brings pleasure to one person, will it bring pleasure to everyone else?

- Can it be wrong to experience pleasure? If so, when?

- Can animals experience pleasure?

- What is pain?

- Does all pain hurt?

- What causes pain?

- What is worse, physical or emotional pain?

- Does something that causes a person to experience pain have the same effect on everyone?

- Is pain caused mostly by people?

- Do some people feel pain more acutely than others?

- Are people brave who don't feel physical pain very much?

- Are people strong who don't feel emotional pain very much?

- Do males and females feel pain equally?

- Should people try to hide their pain?

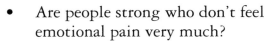

Provocative Proverbs: Pleasure and Pain

A wounded deer leaps highest.

ENGLISH PROVERB

What does this tell us about those who suffer?

_____

Better be wise by the misfortunes of others than by your own.

GREEK PROVERB

What does this proverb have to do with pain?

_____

Only when you have eaten a lemon do you appreciate what sugar is.

UKRAINIAN PROVERB

Comment on this in relation to pleasure and pain.

_____

An hour of pain is as long as a day of pleasure.

ENGLISH PROVERB

What does this mean?

_____

Sweet is pleasure after pain.

ENGLISH PROVERB

Why is pleasure even sweeter when it follows pain?

_____

There is no gathering the rose without being pricked by the thorns.

PERSIAN PROVERB

What warning does this proverb give to those who seek pleasure?

_____

Every cloud has a silver lining.

ENGLISH PROVERB

Why might it be useful for sufferers of pain to know about this proverb?

Debate Topic

We learn more about life by experiencing pain than by experiencing pleasure.

WISDOM

The Ant and the Grasshopper

In a field one summer's day a Grasshopper was hopping about, chirping and singing to its heart's content. An Ant passed by, bearing along with great toil an ear of corn he was taking to the nest.

'Why not come and chat with me,' said the Grasshopper, 'instead of toiling in that way?'

'I am helping to lay up food for the winter,' said the Ant, 'and recommend you to do the same.'

'Why bother about winter?' said the Grasshopper. 'We have got plenty of food at present.'

But the Ant went on its way and continued its toil.

When the winter came the Grasshopper had no food and found itself dying of hunger, while it saw the ants distributing, every day, corn and grain from the stores they had collected in the summer.

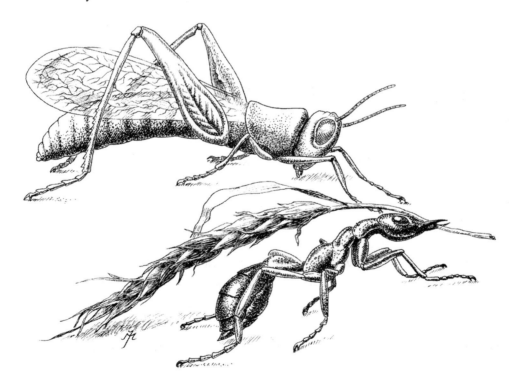

Moral of the story:
It is best to prepare for the days of necessity.

Thinking, Reasoning and Discussing

Question 1. Some people say it is better to live for now (the present) and not to worry about the future. What are your thoughts on this?

....

Question 2. Do you think it is possible to think about and plan for the future too much?

....

Question 3. Would you say that a person who focuses too much on the future might cause their life in the present to suffer? Can you think of examples?

....

Question 4. Do you think that planning for the future requires sacrifices to be made? Justify your answer by giving an example or two.

....

Question 5. What situations or circumstances can you think of that are good examples of 'it is best to prepare for the days of necessity'?

....

Question 6. Most would agree that by planning for the future the Ant shows more *wisdom* than the Grasshopper. Can a person who doesn't plan for the future be considered wise?

....

Question 7. Does being wise mean that you have *always* to do what is best?

....

Question 8. Is a person who follows the best course of action most of the time wise?

....

Question 9. If there are two wise people, can one be wiser than the other? If you think 'yes' can you give an example or two to say how this is possible?

....

Question 10. Is wisdom more about knowledge or decision-making?

....

Question 11. Who is wiser – a person who knows a lot but doesn't often make good decisions, or a person who knows little but usually makes good decisions?

....

Question 12. Can a child have more wisdom than an elderly person?

....

Philosophy in the Classroom © Ron Shaw, Routledge 2008

In 'The Ant and the Grasshopper', the Ant showed its **wisdom** by collecting food for the winter.

Here are some more questions about wisdom to consider:

- What does it mean to be wise?

- Is a wise person wise in *everything*?

- Are wise people *always* correct?

- Can two wise people disagree?

- Is it better to be wise or wealthy?

- Can books make you wise?

- Which is better for obtaining wisdom – reading books, or day-to-day living?

- Can wisdom be taught?

- Is it possible to be wiser than a person who is wise?

- Can a person be totally wise?

Provocative Proverbs: Wisdom

A spoon does not know the taste of soup, nor an educated fool the taste of wisdom.

WELSH PROVERB

What do the Welsh mean by this proverb?

He who builds according to every man's advice will have a crooked house.

DANISH PROVERB

If it is not wise to take everyone's advice, whose advice should we take?

He who has once burnt his mouth always blows his soup.

GERMAN PROVERB

What are the Germans saying here?

The pine stays green in winter... Wisdom stays unchanged in hardship.

CHINESE PROVERB

Why is Wisdom compared to a pine tree?

A teacher is better than two books.

GERMAN PROVERB

Why might this be so?

Better to ask twice than to lose your way once.

DANISH PROVERB

Can you think of a situation where this proverb could apply?

Experience is the mother of wisdom.

WELSH PROVERB

Can you say what this proverb is telling us?

A gram of wisdom is worth more than a kilogram of gold.

ENGLISH PROVERB

We can look at gold and touch it but we can't see or touch wisdom. What other things of value can't we see or touch?

Debate Topic
More wisdom can be gained from books than from day-to-day living.

FRIENDSHIP

The Hare with Many Friends

A Hare was very popular with the other beasts, who all claimed to be her friends. But one day she heard the hounds approaching and hoped to escape them with the aid of her many friends.

So, she went to the horse, and asked him to carry her away from the hounds on his back. But he declined, stating that he had important work to do for his master. He felt sure, he said, that all her other friends would come to her assistance.

She then applied to the bull, and hoped that he would repel the hounds with his horns. The bull replied, 'I am very sorry, but I have an appointment with a lady. But I feel sure that our friend the goat will do what you want.'

The goat, however, feared that his back might do her some harm if he took her upon it. The ram, he felt sure, was the proper friend to apply to.

So she went to the ram and told him the case. The ram replied, 'Another time, my dear friend. I do not like to interfere on the present occasion, as hounds have been known to eat sheep as well as hares.'

The Hare then applied, as a last hope, to the calf, who regretted that he was unable to help her, as he did not like to take the responsibility upon himself, as so many older persons than himself had declined the task. By this time the hounds were quite near, and the Hare took to her heels and luckily escaped.

Moral of the story:
He who has many friends has no friends.

Thinking, Reasoning and Discussing

Question 1. What was the common theme in the excuses of the Hare's friends?

....

Question 2. The Hare had many friends but none seemed to be a **true** friend. What is the difference between a friend and a true friend?

....

....

Question 3. Friendships begin as acquaintances. What is the difference between an acquaintance and a friend? When does an acquaintance become a friend?

....

....

Question 4. Do you think it is easier to have a true friend if you have few friends or many friends?

....

....

Question 5. What do you think is best – having just one friend who is a true friend; or having many friends, none of whom is a true friend? Discuss the advantages and disadvantages of each case.

....

....

Question 6. Can you think of a real-life example of a person being helped by a true friend?

....

Question 7. Is the friendship of a family member the same as the friendship of a non-family member?

....

Question 8. Can a pet be a friend? If so, can every type of pet be a friend?

....

Question 9. If you find yourself in trouble, are you more likely to turn to a family member or a true friend?

....

Philosophy in the Classroom © Ron Shaw, Routledge 2008

In 'The Hare with Many Friends', the Hare realised that true friendship and having many **friends** do not always go together.

Here are some more questions about friendship to consider:

- Can a person be a friend to him/herself?

- How long does it take to become a friend?

- What is needed for two people to be friends?

- What is needed for one person to like another person?

- What is the difference between *liking* someone and having them as a friend?

- What is needed for one person to dislike another person?

- Can you be good friends with someone who doesn't speak your language? If so, how?

- Can animals be friends with one another?

- Can humans and animals be true friends with each other?

- Can friendship be measured? If so, how?

- What makes one friendship stronger than another?

- Can a friendship of six months be as strong as a friendship of six years?

Provocative Proverbs: Friendship

'Stay' is a charming word in a friend's vocabulary.

IRISH PROVERB

Discuss.

An old friend is like a saddled horse.

AFGHAN PROVERB

What do the Afghans mean?

So long as the pot is boiling, friendship will stay warm.

ARABIAN PROVERB

What is meant by 'so long as the pot is boiling'?

Your friend will swallow your mistakes. Your enemy will present them on a plate.

ARABIAN PROVERB

Discuss this proverb. Try to remember a time when a friend 'swallowed your mistakes'.

Tell me your friends, and I'll tell you who you are.

ASSYRIAN PROVERB

Can you think what the Assyrians might mean here?

A friend – one soul, two bodies.

CHINESE PROVERB

What do the Chinese mean in this proverb?

The road to a friend's house is never long.

DANISH PROVERB

Discuss.

Am I not destroying my enemies when I make friends of them?

PROVERB FROM USA

Comment on this well-known proverb.

> ### Debate Topic
> **You should stand by your friends, no matter what they might do wrong.**

FAVOURS

The Lion and the Mouse

A Lion was awakened from sleep by a Mouse running over his face. Rising up angrily, he caught him and was about to kill him, when the Mouse piteously entreated, saying, 'If you would only spare my life, I would be sure to repay your kindness.' The Lion laughed and let him go.

It happened shortly after this that the Lion was caught by some hunters, who bound him by strong ropes to the ground. The Mouse, recognising his roar, came and gnawed the rope with his teeth, and set him free, exclaiming, 'You ridiculed the idea of my ever being able to help you, expecting to receive from me no repayment of your favour. Now you know that it is possible for even a Mouse to bring benefits to a Lion.'

Moral of the story:
No act of kindness, no matter how small, is ever wasted.

Thinking, Reasoning and Discussing

Question 1. Why do you think the Lion laughed?

....

....

Question 2. Do you think the Lion felt superior to the Mouse? If so, why might he have felt this way? How was his attitude modified?

....

....

....

Question 3. Would you say the Lion was kind, arrogant or both?

....

Question 4. Why do you think the Mouse kept his promise?

....

Question 5. The Mouse saved the Lion to return a favour. Can you think of another reason why the Mouse wanted to save the Lion?

....

....

Question 6. Can you think of another situation where a small animal could save the life of a much larger one?

....

....

Question 7. A small child could prove to be a great friend to an older child or adult. Are you able to think of a way this might happen?

....

....

Question 8. Can you think of an example of a favour repaid?

....

....

In 'The Lion and the Mouse', the Mouse repaid the Lion's **favour**.

Here are some more questions about favours to consider:

- What are favours?

- Why do people do favours for others?

- When we do a favour for someone do we expect anything in return?

- For whom do we do favours?

- Do we do favours for strangers as easily as we do them for friends?

- Can a person do too many favours?

- Does doing a favour have any advantages for the favour-giver?

- Can doing a favour have any disadvantages for the favour-giver?

- Should favours *always* be repaid?

- Are some favours better than others?

- If a favour is returned with a favour, is it possible that one of the favours is better (worth more) than the other?

- Are favours only done by humans, or are they also done by animals?

- Do we only do a favour for someone if they ask us to?

- Do you think there are people who do not like receiving favours?

- Do you think there are people who do not like doing favours?

Provocative Proverbs: Favours

The charity that is a trifle to us can be precious to others.
GREEK PROVERB

What do the Greeks mean by this?

He who boasts of a favour bestowed would like it back again.
GREEK PROVERB

Do you understand this proverb?

The profit on a good action is to have done it.
GREEK PROVERB

What could the Greeks have meant here?

One good turn deserves another.
TRADITIONAL ENGLISH PROVERB

Give an example of this proverb from your experience.

> **Debate Topic**
> **A gift goes further than a favour.**

WEALTH

The Miser and His Gold

A Miser sold all that he had and bought a lump of gold. He buried it in a hole in the ground by the side of an old wall and went to look at it daily. One of his workmen observed his frequent visits to the spot and decided to watch his movements. He soon discovered the secret of the hidden treasure. Digging down, he came to the lump of gold, and stole it. The Miser, on his next visit, found the hole empty. He began to tear his hair and to make loud lamentations. A neighbour, seeing him overcome with grief and learning the cause, said, 'Pray do not grieve so, but go and take a stone, and place it in the hole, and fancy that the gold is still lying there. It will do you quite the same service. For when the gold was there, you had it not, as you did not make the slightest use of it.'

Moral of the story:
Wealth unused might as well not exist.

Thinking, Reasoning and Discussing

Question 1. Why do you think the Miser went to look at his gold each day?

....

Question 2. Why did the neighbour say, 'You had it not'?

....

Question 3. What is wealth?

....

....

Question 4. Do you need to have a lot of money to be wealthy? Can a person with no money be wealthy?

....

....

Question 5. The moral of the story is, 'Wealth unused might as well not exist'. Do you think that if the word 'wealth' were replaced with 'talent' it would still be true?

....

Question 6. Do you know anyone who has a talent they don't use?

....

Question 7. Do you have any talents that you don't make full use of?

....

....

Question 8. Who does better – a person with talent that they don't make full use of, or someone with less talent who tries hard?

....

....

Question 9. If someone has talents in many areas should they try to become an expert in just one of these areas, or try to improve a little more in all areas?

....

....

Philosophy in the Classroom © Ron Shaw, Routledge 2008

In 'The Miser and His Gold', the Miser's **wealth** consisted of a lump of gold which he buried near an old wall.

Here are some more questions about wealth to consider:

- What is wealth?

- Is wealth always to do with money?

- Would it be a better world if everyone had the same amount of material wealth?

- Does wealth (money) give power?

- Are wealthy people respected more than poor people?

- What is better – to be wealthy, but uneducated and unwise; or poor, but educated and wise?

- In the future, if money is no longer used, will it still be possible to be wealthy?

- Who is the wealthier, a millionaire in a prosperous country or a person with £100 in a poor country?

- Is a millionaire who lives alone in a jungle wealthy (there is nothing to buy in the jungle)?

- Can wealth bring happiness?

- Can wealth assist health?

- Can wealth bring fame?

- What are some things that money can't buy?

- Do wealthy people look different from poor people?

- Does wealth always come from hard work?

- Do hard workers deserve to be wealthy?

- What brings wealth to people?

- Should wealthy people give some of their money to poor people?

- Can anyone become wealthy?

- Is being wealthy something that everyone would like?

Provocative Proverbs: Wealth

Wealth gets in the way of wisdom.

JAPANESE PROVERB

Can you say what this means?

Rather a piece of bread with a happy heart than wealth with grief.

EGYPTIAN PROVERB

Can wealth help to ease grief?

A happy heart is better than a full purse.

ITALIAN PROVERB

Can a person with an empty purse be happy?

Can an unhappy person be made happy by filling their purse?

A satisfied man is happy even if he is poor; a dissatisfied man is sad even if he is rich.

CHINESE PROVERB

Is it better to be rich and happy or poor and happy?

We'll never know the worth of water till the well goes dry.

SCOTTISH PROVERB

Which do we take for granted, water or money? Which is the more precious?

Debate Topic
All employees in our country should receive the same pay.

SELF-ACCEPTANCE

The Monkey and the Camel

The Beasts of the forest gave a splendid entertainment at which the Monkey stood up and danced. Having vastly delighted the assembly, he sat down amidst universal applause. The Camel, envious of the praises bestowed on the Monkey and desiring to attract for himself the favour of the guests, proposed to stand up in his turn and dance for their amusement. He moved about in so utterly ridiculous a manner that the Beasts, in a fit of indignation, set upon him with clubs and drove him out of the assembly.

Moral of the story:
It is absurd to ape our betters.

Thinking, Reasoning and Discussing

Question 1. Why did the Camel want to dance?

....

Question 2. Why did the Camel look 'ridiculous'?

....

Question 3. What could the Camel have done, other than dancing, to entertain the guests?

....

....

Question 4. If you see someone do something that you would like to be able to do, do you sometimes try to copy them?

....

Question 5. Do people like to copy those who are popular? If so, why?

....

Question 6. In what ways do people copy others?

....

....

Question 7. Is it easier to copy some things than others?

....

Question 8. What are some things about people that are easy to copy?

....

....

Question 9. What are some things about people that are difficult to copy?

....

....

Question 10. Is it wrong to want to be like someone we admire?

....

....

In 'The Monkey and the Camel', the Camel did not possess **self-acceptance** and wanted, instead, to be like the Monkey.

Here are some more questions about self-acceptance to consider:

*   What is self-acceptance?

*   Should people be happy with themselves as they are or should they always try to improve themselves?

*   Can people *really* change who they are?

*   Do you think there are people who would *not* like to change anything about themselves?

*   Do you think there are people who would like to change *everything* about themselves?

*   Who is the better judge of a person – the person him/herself, or someone else?

*   Can a person be happy without self-acceptance?

*   Can a person without self-acceptance do well in life?

*   Is it easier for some people to accept themselves than it is for others?

*   Are people born equal?

Provocative Proverbs: Self-acceptance

No matter how hard you try, the bull will never give milk.
UKRAINIAN PROVERB

An orange never bears a lime.
PROVERB FROM SIERRA LEONE

You can't put a round peg in a square hole.
IRISH PROVERB

You can only take out of a bag what is already in it.
BRAZILIAN PROVERB

These four proverbs seem to be saying much the same thing. Which one(s) best remind(s) us to accept ourselves and not try to be like others?

He who conquers others is strong; he who conquers himself is mighty.
GREEK PROVERB

How does this saying relate to self-acceptance?

Self-trust is the essence of heroism.
PROVERB FROM USA

Why might it be that some people have little self-trust?

What gives people a lot of self-trust?

I am indeed a king because I know how to rule myself.
ITALIAN PROVERB

What is harder, ruling yourself or ruling others?

Be a friend to yourself and others will be so too.
PROVERB FROM USA

Can you see how this could be true? Discuss.

Learn what you are and be such.
GREEK PROVERB

Is it possible to follow this creed while trying to improve yourself?

Debate Topic
We should never try to be like our heroes.

PURSUING DREAMS

The Milk-woman and Her Pail

A farmer's daughter was carrying her pail of milk from the field to the farmhouse, when she fell a-musing. 'The money for which this milk will be sold, will buy at least three hundred eggs. The eggs, allowing for all mishaps, will produce two hundred and fifty chickens. The chickens will become ready for the market when poultry will fetch the highest price, so that by the end of the year I shall have money enough from my share to buy a new gown. In this dress I will go to the Christmas parties, where all the young fellows will propose to me, but I will toss my head and refuse them every one.' At this moment she tossed her head in unison with her thoughts. Down fell the milk pail to the ground, and all her imaginary schemes perished in a moment.

Moral of the story:
Do not count your chickens before they are hatched.

Thinking, Reasoning and Discussing

Question 1. Do you think the farmer's daughter was unlucky, foolish or careless?

....

Question 2. Why do you think she said, 'I will toss my head and refuse them every one'?

....

Question 3. Do you think the girl would have a better chance of doing well in life if she didn't 'count her chickens before they are hatched'?

....

Question 4. Some would say she was making plans for her future and that this was wise of her. What do you think?

....

....

Question 5. Do you think the girl would have been better planning ahead in smaller steps?

....

....

Question 6. Is it better to plan a little way ahead or far ahead?

....

....

Question 7. Do you have a future plan or ambition? If so, are you making small steps to achieve it?

....

....

Question 8. Is it wise or unwise to 'count your chickens before they are hatched'? Explain your answer with an example.

....

....

In 'The Milk-woman and Her Pail', the farmer's daughter was taking the first step in **pursuing her dream**.

Here are some more questions about pursuing dreams and goals to consider:

- Are 'dreams' and 'goals' the same thing?

- Does *everyone* have dreams and goals?

- Is it good to have dreams and goals?

- Do you 'fail' if you don't realise your dream?

- Why do people set goals for themselves?

- Can we be successful without setting ourselves goals?

- Do we need to plan in order to achieve our goals?

- Is it better to aim a bit higher or a bit lower than what we think we can achieve?

- Consider a person who achieves their goals. Does this mean they are successful in life?

- Consider a person who *doesn't* achieve their goals. Does this mean they are unsuccessful in life?

- Do you need to be talented in order to realise your dream or goals?

- Does luck play a part in the realisation of dreams and the achievement of goals?

- Do people need to work hard in order to realise their dreams and achieve their goals?

- Are those who have dreams and goals more likely to be successful than those who don't have them?

- Do we need others to help us realise our dreams and achieve our goals?

- Do we need to know our capabilities before setting goals for ourselves?

Provocative Proverbs: Pursuing Dreams

If you can walk, you can dance. If you can talk, you can sing.
ZIMBABWEAN PROVERB

What is this saying about a person's capabilities?

Fall seven times, stand up eight.
JAPANESE PROVERB

What advice does this give about pursuing our dreams and goals?

It's not enough to know how to ride – you must also know how to fall.
MEXICAN PROVERB

What does this say about pursuing dreams and goals?

You cannot unscramble eggs.
NORTH AMERICAN PROVERB

What does this say about the mistakes a person makes?

When the apple is ripe it will fall.
IRISH PROVERB

Can you see that this is saying something about patience?

Never let your feet run faster than your shoes.
SCOTTISH PROVERB

Discuss this in relation to pursuing your goals.

Nothing ventured, nothing gained.
ENGLISH PROVERB

Discuss.

Debate Topic
Without a dream you'll never be successful.

SELF-RELIANCE

The Lark and Her Young Ones

A Lark had made her nest in the early spring on the young green wheat. The brood had almost grown to their full strength and attained the use of their wings and the full plumage of their feathers, when the owner of the field, looking over his ripe crop, said, 'The time has come when I must ask all my neighbours to help me with my harvest.' One of the young Larks heard his speech and related it to his mother, inquiring of her where they should move for safety. 'There is no occasion to move yet, my son,' she replied. 'The man who only sends to his friends to help him with his harvest is not really in earnest.' The owner of the field came again a few days later and saw the wheat shedding the grain from excess of ripeness. He said, 'I will come myself tomorrow with my labourers, and with as many reapers as I can hire, and will get in the harvest.' The Lark, on hearing these words, said to her brood, 'It is time now to be off, my little ones, for the man is in earnest this time; he no longer trusts his friends, but will reap the field himself.'

Moral of the story:
Self-help is the best help.

Thinking, Reasoning and Discussing

Question 1. Why did the mother Lark think that the farmer wasn't in earnest the first time he appeared?

....

Question 2. Why might the farmer have wanted his neighbours to help?

....

Question 3. Why might the farmer's neighbours have declined to help?

....

Question 4. When the farmer finally decided to harvest the field the wheat was over-ripe. Meanwhile his neighbours had probably finished harvesting their fields. Is this a case of a trusting farmer with unhelpful neighbours or a foolish farmer with wise neighbours?

....

Question 5. When was a time you benefited from a friend's help? Did this help make things easier for you? Could you have got by equally well on your own?

....

....

Question 6. Think of a time when you helped a friend. Do you think the friend could have got by just as well without your help?

....

Question 7. If someone is in need of help, are you more likely to help if they are a friend? Explain.

....

....

Question 8. Why is it easier to seek the help of a friend than that of a stranger?

....

Question 9. When is it better to seek the help of others rather than attempt something by yourself?

....

Question 10. When is it better to attempt something yourself rather than seek the help of others?

....

In 'The Lark and Her Young Ones', the owner of the field found that he had to **rely on himself** and put in an effort of his own.

Here are some more questions about self-reliance to consider:

- What is meant by self-reliance?

- Is it good to be self-reliant?

- Should all people be self-reliant?

- Should we always rely on ourselves?

- Do you need self-confidence to be self-reliant?

- Can self-reliance be taught?

- What is effort?

- Can making an effort *ever* be bad?

- Should we make more efforts for ourselves or for others?

- Is it wrong to make efforts for others but not for ourselves?

- Does effort bring reward? If yes, does it *always* bring reward?

- Are there times when we should make no effort?

- What is the opposite of effort?

- Do some people need to make more effort than others?

- What determines the amount of effort a person needs to make?

- Is there ever a limit to how much effort we should make?

Provocative Proverbs: Self-reliance

Success and rest don't sleep together.
RUSSIAN PROVERB

To try and fail is not laziness.
PROVERB FROM SIERRA LEONE

Which of these proverbs is the most creative/clever? Why?

_____

Better to wear out shoes than sheets.
SCOTTISH PROVERB

What is being said here?

_____

By trying often, the monkey learns to jump from the tree.
PROVERB FROM CAMEROON

Is this about persistence, ability or both? Explain.

_____

If you have planted a tree you must water it too.
SRI LANKAN PROVERB

Give some examples to show that you know what this means.

_____

When a needle falls into a deep well, many people will look into the well, but few will be ready to go down after it.
PROVERB FROM REPUBLIC OF GUINEA

Try to work out what this saying is all about.

_____

If you do not sow in the spring you will not reap in the autumn.
IRISH PROVERB

Is this about planning, effort or both? Explain.

> **Debate Topic**
> **It is wrong to rely on others, even family and friends.**

BEAUTY

The Peacock and Juno

A Peacock once placed a petition before Juno, desiring to have the voice of a nightingale in addition to his other attractions. But Juno refused his request. When he persisted, and pointed out that he was her favourite bird, she said, 'You have an appearance which other birds envy. Be content with your lot.'

Moral of the story:
One cannot be first in everything.

Thinking, Reasoning and Discussing

Question 1. Why do you think Juno (Queen of the Gods) refused the peacock's request?

....

....

Question 2. Which would be better – being the most beautiful bird, or being the bird with the most beautiful song?

....

Question 3. Which three of these words best describe the peacock: vain, satisfied, arrogant, modest, humble, greedy?

....

Question 4. What is better – to be first in one thing and not very good in everything else, or to be average in everything?

....

....

Question 5. Do you think everybody is good at something?

....

....

Question 6. It is true that a person cannot be first in everything. However, some people are lucky to be first in more than one thing. Can there be disadvantages to being first in many things?

....

....

Question 7. Is it better to concentrate on improving our strengths or improving our weaknesses?

....

....

Question 8. If you could be first in one thing what would that be, and why?

....

....

Question 9. Is it better to be satisfied with what you are or to try to be the best?

....

....

In 'The Peacock and Juno', the Peacock wasn't satisfied being the bird with the most **beauty**.

Here are some more questions about beauty to consider:

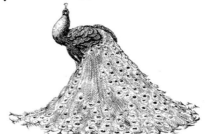

- What is meant by beauty?

- How is beauty different from appearance?

- What are examples of beauty?

- What is the opposite of beauty?

- What gives something beauty? Who determines beauty?

- Is beauty the same for everyone?

- Can something ever be beautiful to one person and ugly to another?

- Is there such a thing as a beautiful thought? If yes, give an example.

- What is meant by a beautiful mind?

- Can things lose their beauty? If so, how?

- Can non-beautiful things become beautiful?

- Does the term 'beautiful person' have more than one meaning?

- Can people create *things* of beauty?

- Why is it that people don't always agree on what is beautiful?

- Consider two beautiful flowers. Does it make sense to say that one is more beautiful than the other? If so, how can something be more beautiful than what is already beautiful?

- Can you think of anything that is *always* beautiful? Would everyone agree?

- Name some things that can *never* be beautiful. Would everyone agree?

- If one person says, 'That dog is beautiful' and ninety-nine people disagree with him/her, who is right?

- If everyone (and every animal) were blind, would there still be things in the world that have a beautiful appearance?

Provocative Proverbs: Beauty

Beauty is in the eye of the beholder.

ENGLISH PROVERB

Say what this means and give an example.

A beautiful thing is never perfect.

EGYPTIAN PROVERB

Do you agree with this? Justify your answer.

Better to have a diamond with a few small flaws than a rock that is perfect.

INDIAN PROVERB

Can something with a flaw be perfect? Back up your answer by providing an example or two.

Beauty without wisdom is like a flower in the mud.

ROMANIAN PROVERB

Why do you think the Romanians make this comparison?

A light is still a light, even though the blind man cannot see it.

AUSTRIAN PROVERB

What might a blind man say is beautiful?

Put silk on a goat, and it's still a goat.

IRISH PROVERB

Does this mean that something can't be made beautiful or that something can't be made to *look* beautiful? Is there a difference?

> ## Debate Topic
> **Beautiful sights give more pleasure than beautiful sounds.**